Wandering Woman: Illinois
The Ultimate Road Trip: One Woman's Journey Across the United States by RV

Julie Bettendorf

Contents

Introduction

"Not all who wander are lost." JRR Tolkien

Are you sure? I thought to myself, as I tried not to panic. I was a long way from anything familiar, but that was how it should be. I had driven thousands of miles on dusty, pothole-filled roads. It's often on the worst roads that you can discover something truly amazing.

My dusty CRV was parked beside me, containing one restless dog and a variety of snack bags, all empty by now. There were no buildings in sight, no cars or people or movement at all. Only the constant humming of the insects as they buzzed around my head.

I turned to my left – another straight road that trailed off into the distance. I glanced over to the right, then behind me – two more barely discernible roads stretched out into the abyss. I was in a four-way intersection with no signs, no sense of direction, and no sign of life for several miles. No cell service either. *Damn*, I thought. *I'm lost.*

How did I get here? I couldn't help but feel like this little intersection was a cruel metaphor for life. I began to daydream, imagining each road might transport me back to a different time, a different role in my life, and a different me.

If I took the road from whence I came, it could lead me all the way back to Oregon, back to my cheating third husband, back to a life of loneliness and solitude. There is no greater loneliness than being married to someone who isn't actually present in your life.

If I took the road to my left, perhaps it could take me back to my career as a dental hygienist, a job I hated deep down in my soul. There is something so disengaging about cleaning teeth for a living. It's a disgusting, smelly way to get a paycheck. It pays well, which is great, but the best part is the huge gob of friends I enjoy to this day.

Or maybe the road to my right, *yes – maybe that's the path*, I imagined. Maybe it could take me back to my real treasure, my kids. Back to their smiling, innocent faces as toddlers, as they danced around the Christmas tree and their father and I were still married. Back when they still needed me for every little thing.

But, that was just it. I didn't feel needed anymore. My kids weren't toddlers anymore – they were both full-grown adults, and far too busy for me. My dental buddies were still working, but I wasn't. Dental hygiene had robbed me of the cartilage in my fingers, giving me severe, disabling arthritis. And, I wouldn't be returning to any more husbands either, because three marriages were quite enough for me.

All three of these paths, all three of these roles – the wife, the mother, and the dental hygienist – had seemingly been stripped from me within a year. I was lost and looking to find myself again.

The funny thing about this phrase, "not all who wander are lost" – is that, in my experience, wandering and being lost walk hand-in-hand with one another, and the expression can be flipped. In my experience, not all who are lost are wandering, and that is a real disservice to the beauty and clarity that the world has to offer.

When one becomes lost, wandering is the only option to guide oneself back to a path. After all, one could not come upon any dirt path at all without wandering.

I began wandering at an early age, both with my mind and with my feet. At eight years old, I was reading a book about archaeology and dreaming of one day seeing Egypt. I didn't follow a traditional path in high school either, going heavily into foreign languages, in hopes of one day using them.

At twenty-five years old, I divorced my first husband (the dental student who talked me into becoming a dental hygienist so I could work for him) and decided to give traveling a real shot. I took off for the Andes and Macchu Picchu, climbing up ancient Inca stone steps to reach the magnificent ruins.

Anyone who has been to Macchu Picchu will tell you there is something ethereal and deeply spiritual about the place. The ruins stretch out across the emerald green mountains, way up in the middle of the sky. Macchu Picchu gave me my first experience of feeling history. This trip inspired me to come back and complete a degree in archaeology, and I've been wandering ever since.

More travel followed including a backpack trip around Europe for three months, by myself, and trips to Britain, Italy, and Greece. I visited the burial places of Crusaders, mummies, and ancient kings. I happened upon the castle of my namesake in Bettendorf, Luxembourg, and wandered my way through European history.

My favorite excursion by far was finally seeing Egypt with my daughter in 2012. Just like my childhood dream envisioned, I rode a camel beneath the pyramids of Giza, with my head wrapped in some man's sweaty turban. It was perfect.

Traveling has always been my own personal antidote to pain. I went to Mexico after my first and second divorces, Canada after my third, and Italy after my dad died. Call it avoidance if you want, but I call it an accelerated form of healing in the purest sense of the word. I believe travel can heal your soul.

Wandering has always worked its wonders on me – made me feel renewed, rejoiceful, grateful, and purposeful. It's been my medicine.

So, as I stood in that intersection, I once again wondered how wandering had led me so astray this time. *What the hell am I supposed to do now?* It was then that I realized that one last path had not been considered yet – the path which stretched straight out in front of me. *Which role does this represent?* I pondered.

The answer smacked me in the face.

That last dirt road – the only path that could take me where I wanted to go, the only path that ever truly healed me or showed me the way – was the path of the traveler. The wife, the mother, and the hygienist roles – though valued in their time – were sitting in the bleachers now. It was time to welcome and enable my boldest, bravest, and perhaps most pivotal role yet:

The role of the Wandering Woman.

Welcome to Wandering Woman

This book is for you – the grieving empty nester mom, the begrudged housewife, the woman in need of a drastic change in her life. Really, this book is for anyone with a passion for traveling. If you feel lost with no sense of direction or purpose in life, that's a bonus – this book will be even more appealing to you. And lastly, if you're a man reading this book, congratulations for holding a book with the word woman in the title. You're contributing to gender equality, and that's pretty neat.

I decided to combine three of my dearest loves – travel, history, and archaeology – and put them into a book because I believe wandering has the power to change your life. I have been to many areas of the world and have enjoyed too many outstanding experiences to list. However, by the time both my children moved out in 2017, I realized I was a stranger in my own country. It was the perfect time to explore a new country (my own) and discover a new me at the same time. I have been traveling for seven years now, and I've upgraded to a small RV. I also have a new traveling companion, another sweet Sheltie, named Rosie. *Wandering Woman* is the chronicle of my journey across the United States, discovering the joy of getting lost and finding myself along the way.

Why You Need to Take a Road Trip

A *merica, the beautiful?* I sure think so, but I didn't realize just how beautiful our country is until I embarked on traveling across the United States, full time, in a small RV.

The United States offers something for everyone. From spectacular beaches, austere mountains, to rolling plains, our country has it all. It's difficult to comprehend just how large and impressive our scenery is, until you experience it first-hand, with the ultimate road trip.

I also realized just how much of our history is missing from U.S. history I was taught as a kid. The history of our country didn't begin with the pilgrims landing on Plymouth Rock in the 1600s. Our history is far more ancient, with rock art and archaeological sites dating back over 12,000 years.

We owe a tremendous debt to early pioneers who tamed our land. The Mormons and other groups ventured into the great unknown with their families and their worldly possessions. Some of them pulled cumbersome handcarts across the country to settle in inhospitable, dangerous locations.

The goal of **Wandering Woman** is to bring history back to life and make it interesting again. I am presenting some famous sites, and many little-known ones. You will take the road-less-traveled with me, while we explore ghost towns, rock art sites, archaeological sites, and museums, to discover the colorful tapestry that is our country.

I present some history, including dates, but my goal is to present more of the real-life stories of history, including ghost stories, profiles in history, voices from the past, and moments in time, to give you, the reader, a deeper understanding of the context of history.

This is by no means an exhaustive list of places to visit. In fact, I encourage you to discover America for yourself, as I am doing, by making a trek across the land by car or RV. You can venture forth as the early explorers did, just a little more comfortably, with a lot less hardship.

I hope you enjoy this book and take a little time out to discover our beautiful country, and maybe even discover yourself in the process.

Safe Travels,

Julie Bettendorf

Welcome to Illinois

The Prairie State

I llinois is a fascinating state with something for everyone. Abra-ham Lincoln lived there. You can experience his early years in New Salem, when Lincoln first came to Illinois. The courthouse where he practiced law is also in Illinois. You can also discov-er early Native American history by exploring mounds sites like Dickson, and world-famous Cahokia. When you come to Illinois, take some time to see it all.

Five Things to Love about Illinois:

- Picturesque riverfront towns like Galena

- Massive Native American mounds like Cahokia

- Abraham Lincoln history from sites like New Salem

- Early French settlement from sites like Fort de Chartres

- Pioneer structures like the Halfway Tavern

Dreams of Illinois

"If you don't like the weather, wait fifteen minutes." **Ralph Kiner**

"I have a doctorate in fine arts from Knox College in Illinois. All I did was give a speech, and now everybody has to call me Dr. Colbert." **Stephen Colbert**

"The thing about Chicago is that it really isn't like any other place. The architecture and the layout of the city are the best. I'm from the Midwest, and consider myself a Midwesterner. I feel most at home there. I love California. I have great friends in California. I just have always considered Illinois to be home." **Vince Vaughn**

Famous Illinois Citizens

Abraham Lincoln, 16th president of the United States, 1809-1865

Betty White, comedian and actress, 1922-2021

Walt Disney, animator and producer, 1901-1966

Ernest Hemingway, writer, 1899-1961

John Belushi, comedian and actor, 1949-1982

Harrison Ford, actor, born in 1942

Bob Newhart, comedian and actor, 1929-2024

Robin Williams, comedian and actor, 1951-2014

Early Illinois

Old Cemetery, Galena

Early Bishop Hill

Union Soldier from Illinois

Galena

B eautiful *Galena* began as La Pointe, which became the town
of Galena in 1826. The town is picturesque, and the people

are very friendly. I could spend weeks or months in Galena and never tire of it.

Mining equipment, supplies, and people floated down the river to Galena. The small town became an impressive city, when Chicago was still a village. Galena's wealth began to show itself in the 1840s, when stately mansions began to appear.

Today, you can see many of these elaborate mansions. Including Dowling House, built in 1826, and DeSoto House Hotel, which was opened in 1855. You can also visit the 1897 blacksmith shop, which was one of 35 blacksmith shops once serving Galena. My favorite is this magnificent structure, the Stillman Mansion, built in 1858.

Galena is also famous because the home of Ulysses S. Grant is there. The home was built in 1860, and it was gifted to Grant when he came home from the Civil War.

Grant originally worked in his family's tanning shop but when war began, he left to go fight for the Union. The Grant family owned the house until Grant died in 1885. His wife, Julia, died in 1902. The Grant children gave the house back to Galena in 1904. 90 percent of the furnishings are original.

Shops, eateries, and historic buildings are everywhere. If you crave a hometown experience, Galena needs to be on your bucket list. Galena could be everyone's hometown.

How to get to Galena:

Galena is located in Northwestern Illinois, about a 3 hour drive from Chicago.

Profiles in history:

Ulysses S. Grant was born on April 27, 1822, in Point Pleasant, Ohio. He grew up going to private schools and eventually attended West Point. Grant was stationed in Missouri, where he met Julia Dent. He married her in 1848, and they had four children.

Grant fought in the Mexican-American War and later in the Civil War, becoming a brigadier general. He fought at the Battle of Shiloh, and then Vicksburg. His brilliant tactics eventually led to the surrender of Robert E. Lee's Confederate armies at Appomattox, ending the Civil War on April 9, 1865.

He became the 18th president of the United States, serving from 1869 to 1877. In 1884, Grant developed throat cancer. He decided to write his memoirs to help raise funds for his family. The memoirs sold for about $450,000. Ulysses S. Grant died on July 23, 1885.

A word about mining terms and superstitions:

Some common terms thrown about in the world of mining include:

Prospecting-looking for material to be mined, usually in the form of a gold or silver vein trapped within quartz. This is known as "blossom rock."

Placer mining-to find superficial deposits of gold in streams and rivers

Lode mining-to find deposits of precious metals enclosed in rock

Miners worked in extremely hazardous conditions, and the danger of their jobs may have led them to become highly superstitious. These are just a few of the superstitions miners believed in:

Women were bad luck in the mines, especially if the woman was a redhead. It meant someone would die.

Someone would also die if a black cat or a dog entered the mine.

Whistling in a mine drove away good spirits and invited bad ones. Whistling was also believed to cause vibrations in the earth, prompting a cave-in.

A cave-in was most likely to happen between midnight and 4 AM.

Miners would often quit a day early because they believed they would be injured or killed on their last shift (Park City Museum, Utah)

Bishop Hill

L ovely ***Bishop Hill*** was founded in 1846 by Swedish religious
dissenters who chose to view the Bible as the only book of

God. The settlers arrived in the fall of 1846 after walking 160 miles from Chicago.

They dug shelters of half cave and half timber, fitting as many as thirty people sleeping in bunks. and spent the winter. 96 settlers died that first winter. Permanent buildings were begun in 1847, reaching a total of 20 buildings.

The leader of the dissenters was Erik Jansson, who was impris-
oned by the state church of Sweden. Jansson was murdered in
1850, shot by a defector from the colony. Jansson was 41 when
he died. After his death, the community was run by a board of
trustees.

Bishop Hill prospered until 1861, when the Civil War and money mismanagement led to the colony dissolution in 1861. Some men went off to fight for the Union, while others left for California, searching for gold.

Today you can enjoy several historic buildings, including the Colony Church, built in 1848. The sanctuary was on second floor. The first floor and basement were apartments, sometimes housing as many as 10 people per apartment. This is an example of what an apartment looked like.

The church contains a fine museum with artifacts from the period of the settlers, including these bricks, made and decorated by members of the Colony.

Other buildings include the Colony Hotel, built in the mid 1850s, the Colony Store, built in 1853, and the Colony Hospital built in 1855.

How to get to Bishop Hill:

Bishop Hill is located about 45 miles northwest of Peoria.

Dickson Mounds

The **Dickson Mounds** is a serene, peaceful Native American site overlooking the Illinois River. The site gets its name from chiropractor Don Dickson, who began excavations in 1927.

The site was established before 800 AD and was used until short-
ly after 1250 AD. It contains ten burial mounds and a platform
mound. At its peak, it was a large burial area with at least two
cemeteries. It is estimated that at least 3000 people are buried at
Dickson Mounds.

The people who lived at Dickson Mounds underwent a major change. The early hunter-gatherers of 950-1050 AD enjoyed better health than those of the later inhabitants. The skeletons from this period ate a mixed, nutritious diet contributing to strength and bone density.

The hunter-gatherers were replaced by an agrarian lifestyle with significant farming. Skeletons from this period indicate dental issues, spinal conditions, and other health conditions. Over 800 skeletons were examined in the study.

During excavations, a group of four skeletons were uncovered, with their heads missing. The heads were replaced by pots. This is believed to be a sacrificial event.

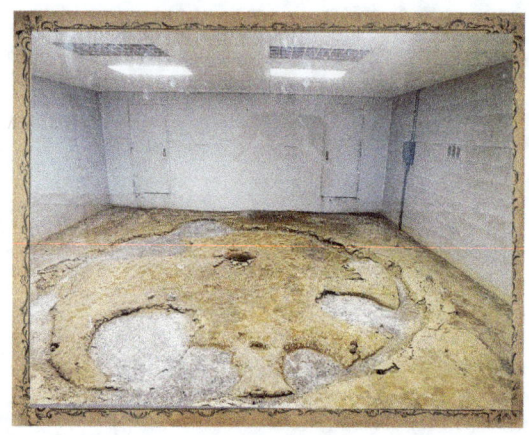

Other skeletal evidence indicates a period of violence occurring about 1300 AD. Skeletons from this period show evidence of broken bones, scalping cuts, stab wounds, and arrow points still in bone.

Don Dickson eventually opened a museum, unfortunately featuring 237 skeletons on display for curious patrons. His museum was closed in 1992. The current museum displays a fascinating collection of artifacts excavated in the mounds.

One of my favorite artifacts is this human head effigy, most likely worn as an ornament by a warrior.

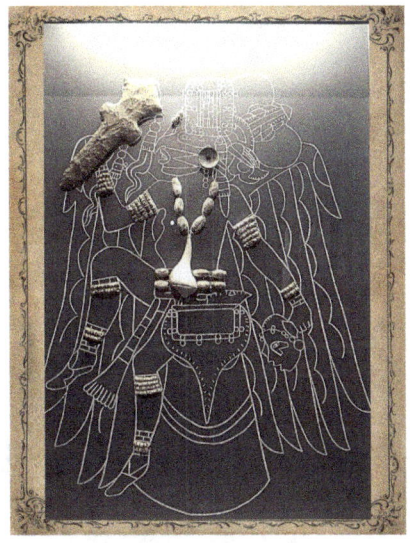

Warriors wore many ornaments including copper ear spools, copper medallions, and shell jewelry.

One of the more poignant exhibits is that of domesticated dog skeletons which date to 8500 years ago. They were buried deliberately and are some of the oldest remains of domesticated dogs in the world.

How to get to Dickson Mounds:

The Dickson Mounds are located at 10956 N. Dickson Mounds Rd. in Lewistown.

A helpful timeline of early Illinois culture:

There are several identifiable cultural periods unique to Illinois. Cultural periods are determined by artifacts present at the site, methods of subsistence such as hunter-gatherer or farming, and establishment of structures for housing and temples. These are the timelines present in Illinois archaeological sites:

The Paleo Indian Period, which lasted from 10,000 to 8,000 BC

The Illinois Archaic Period, which lasted from 8000 to 600 BC

The Woodland Period, which lasted from 600 BC to 1050 AD

The Mississippian Period, which lasted from 1050 to 1450 AD

The Proto-Historic Period, which lasted from 1450 to 1673 AD

The Historic Period, which was after 1673 AD

A word about cultures, traditions, and periods

A culture is a specific social group with a unique way of life. An example is the Adena culture, identified by conical burial mounds, copper artifacts, and specific shapes of beads and pipes.

A tradition, is a broadly identified way of life, in use by different cultures at different time periods. The Woodland Tradition can be identified across many cultures in many geographic locations. Woodland tradition is identified by the beginning of agriculture, potter making, and the establishment of permanent villages.

A period, is a specified span of time during which one tradition is dominant. The Woodland Tradition has several periods including the burial mound period of 1000 BC to 700 AD. A period is a method of measuring time.

Old Lincoln Courtroom

The ***Old Lincoln Courthouse*** is located in Beardstown, a town founded in 1819 by Thomas Beard. The town was platted in 1829.

Abraham Lincoln first came to Beardstown in 1832, about 13 years after it was settled. Lincoln lived in New Salem, about 35 miles away. He worked as a steamboat pilot, transporting goods along the Sangamon River, from New Salem to Beardstown, and back again.

In April 1832, Lincoln served in the Black Hawk War, and became captain of his company. After serving in the military, Lincoln became a lawyer and practiced law in the courthouse in Beardstown.

The imposing building known as the "Almanac Trial" courthouse, was built in 1844. The upstairs houses the courtroom where Lincoln defended 24-year-old William "Duff" Armstrong. It's the only courtroom where Lincoln practiced law, that is still in use today.

The courthouse building also houses the original jail where Duff Armstrong was incarcerated.

As you walk around the courthouse, don't miss the 1857 Almanac, similar to the one Lincoln used at the trial.

One of the most fascinating items in the courthouse is a portrait of Lincoln himself, taken in 1858. He is dressed in a white suit, a color which Lincoln disliked to wear.

How to get to the Old Lincoln Courthouse:

The Old Lincoln Courthouse is located at 101 West 3rd Street in Beardstown.

A moment in time:

On May 7, 1858, Lincoln participated in an important case. A man named James Metzker was beaten on August 29, 1857 and he died. William Armstrong and James Morris were charged with the crime. Armstrong was the son of one of Lincoln's good friends, so Lincoln represented him.

Norris had been found guilty the previous year. Witness Charles Allen said he saw the murder by the light of the moon. Lincoln held out a copy of an 1857 almanac showing that the moon could not have illuminated the scene, because the moon was already low in the west. Lincoln appealed to the jurors, saying:

"He was once a poor, friendless boy, that Armstrong's father took him into his house, fed and clothed him, and gave him a home."

Lincoln had tears in his eyes as he spoke. Armstrong was acquitted of the crime.

New Salem

*N**ew Salem*** was founded in 1829, and it was the home of Abraham Lincoln from 1831 to 1837. The first lot in New

Salem was sold for $12.50. New Salem reached its peak population in 1832, and was abandoned by 1840.

Many of the original settlers moved to Springfield and the surrounding areas. It was deserted for over 60 years, until the land was purchased by William Randolph Hearst in 1906. Active reconstruction began in 1932.

The Henry Onstot Residence was the home of Henry Onstott, the town cooper. The house was built in 1835, and contains sparse, but comfortable furnishings.

The Cooper Shop of Henry Onstott is the only original building from New Salem. Onstot made buckets, tubs, and barrels which cost 40 cents for a flour barrel and $1.00 dollar for a meat barrel. Wash tubs and well buckets cost $1.50 each.

The Tavern was built in 1828 and offered lodging fixed at 37.5 cents per day for a meal and one night's stay.

The Martin Waddell Residence, built in 1832, housed Waddell, his wife, one son, and several daughters. Waddell was a hatter, creating rabbit fur hats for 50 cents, coonskin hats for $2, and wool felt hats.

Dr. John Allen had a residence in New Salem, built in 1831. Allen began a temperance society and held meetings in his home. He also taught Sunday school inside his house.

Children learned in the schoolhouse by memorization and recitation, so Lincoln called it a "blab" school.

Isaac Burner moved to New Salem in 1832, purchased two lots for $10 and built the residence where he and his family would live.

The First Berry-Lincoln Store was opened in 1831, by James and Rowan Herndon. They sold their interests to William Berry and Lincoln, who bought his interest with a promissory note.

You can also visit the Second Berry-Lincoln Store across the street. New Salem had several stores, selling liquor for 12 to 25 cents per half pint. Stores were also gathering places, and the source of entertainment because gander pulls, cock fights, and wrestling matches were also held there.

The reconstructed village of New Salem is impressive, and so are the serenely beautiful grounds. I loved the many horses quietly grazing. It's a beautiful spot.

How to get to New Salem:

New Salem is located at 15588 History Lane, in Petersburg, Illinois.

Voices from the past:

"He was dressed in a pair of blue jeans trousers indefinitely rolled up, a cotton shirt, striped white and blue,....and a buckeye chip hat for which a demand of twelve and a half cents would have been exorbitant." **Description of Abraham Lincoln, age 22, as he piloted a flatboat into New Salem in 1831.**

Profiles in history:

Abraham Lincoln was born in a log cabin in Kentucky on February 12, 1809, and grew up in poverty on the frontier. Lincoln was a lifelong lover of animals, having cats, dogs, and horses throughout his life. He educated himself, eventually becoming a lawyer. He walked the 20 miles from New Salem to John Stuart's law office in Springfield, to borrow law books. Lincoln moved to Springfield in April, 1837, riding a borrowed horse, with all of his possessions packed in saddlebags. He became the 16th president of the United States in 1861. After the election, several of the states condoning slavery seceded from the Union, creating the Confederate States. A month after Lincoln became president, the Confederacy attacked Fort Sumter, and the Civil War began. Abraham Lincoln was assassinated five days after the Confederate armies surrendered at Appomattox, on April 14, 1865. He was attending a play at Ford's Theatre in Washington, D.C.

Lincoln Family Home

T he ***Lincoln Family Home*** in Springfield is the house where Abraham Lincoln and his family lived from 1844 to 1861, before he became president of the United States. Lincoln moved to Springfield from New Salem in 1837. Lincoln met his wife Mary Todd in Springfield and they married in 1842.

Abraham and Mary bought the house in 1844 from Reverend Dresser for $1500, and It was the only home Lincoln would ever own. Three children were born there, and one of the children, Eddie, died in the house.

The house has twelve rooms, including a parlor, kitchen, parents bedroom, and boys bedroom, which are spread over two floors. It has been restored to how it looked in 1860. There are artifacts throughout the house, including this charming wooden pull toy, made by Lincoln sometime between 1845 and 1855.

Don't miss the other historic houses around the Lincoln Home, including the Dean House and the Arnold House.

How to get to the Lincoln Family Home:

The Lincoln Family Home is located at 413 South 8th Street, in Springfield.

Profiles in history:

Mary Todd Lincoln was born in Lexington, Kentucky on December 13, 1818, into wealth and privilege. She was well educated. Mary later moved to Springfield. Mary was once courted by Stephen Douglas, a political opponent of Abraham Lincoln. Mary met Abraham when he was still a struggling lawyer, and they became engaged. Several members of Mary's family disapproved of the match, due to Lincoln's lower status. They married on November 4, 1842. The Lincolns had four children, all boys. Only one of their children survived their parents. Mary was seated next to Abraham when he was shot in Ford's Theatre on April 14, 1865.

Ghost story:

The **Lincoln Family Home** may be haunted. There are stories of a female spirit haunting the house, which has been seen by staff members. One staff member stated that she saw Lincoln's rocking chair rock back and forth, objects moving to different parts of the house, and she experienced being tapped on the shoulder by an unseen hand.

Visitors to the house have also had paranormal experiences. Some have heard voices coming from empty rooms, feeling cold spots, and seeing the rocking chair rock back and forth. Another visitor said he saw a female figure standing in the parlor. The figure was Mary Lincoln.

Cahokia Village

*C**ahokia Village*** began as a French Mission, established by
Father Pinet in 1689. He was tasked with converting the
Cahokian and Tamaroa Native Americans to Christianity.

French Canadian colonists later founded the village in 1696 as a Catholic mission. The Church of the Holy Family is the oldest Catholic parish in the United States which is still active. In 1776, a bell was given to the church by King Louis XV.

Cahokia Village would become one of the largest French colonial settlements in Illinois County. At its peak, the village contained 3000 people.

The area including Cahokia Village declined as a result of the French and Indian War in 1763. Cahokia and the surrounding area became part of the United States in 1783, as part of the Treaty of Paris. It was initially designated part of the Northwest Territory. Cahokia later became part of the Illinois Territory, when Ohio and Indiana became states.

Other important buildings in the area are the Cahokia Courthouse, built around 1740, and the Jarrot Mansion, built in 1810 for
Frenchman Nicholas Jarrot. The Jarrot Mansion is the oldest brick
building in Illinois.

How to get to Cahokia Village:

Cahokia Village is located in Collinsville, Illinois, across the Mississippi River from St. Louis, Missouri.

Profiles in history:

Nicholas Jarrot was born in France in 1764. At the age of 27, he joined a group of priests sailing to America. He became a prominent resident of Cahokia in 1793. He bought land amassing to 25,000 acres, including the Cahokia Mounds and Lewis and Clark's winter campsite. Jarrot became a lawyer, judge, and captain of the militia. He built the mansion at Cahokia Village for his wife, Julie St. Gemme de Beauvais, who was the daughter of patriots of the American Revolution. Jarrot developed a fever and died on December 8, 1820.

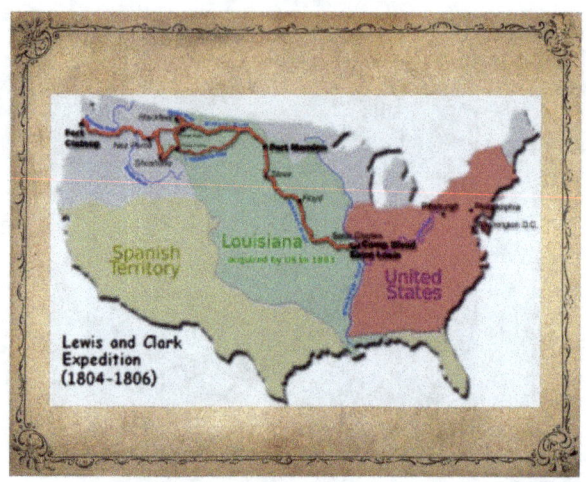

A word about Lewis & Clark's Corp of Discovery:

In 1803, President Thomas Jefferson funded the expedition with $2500. The group was to find the most direct water route to the Pacific. Meriwether Lewis, who was a family friend of Jefferson was put in charge of the expedition. He enlisted his friend from the Indian campaigns, William Clark.

Meriwether Lewis and his men left Pittsburgh on 8/31/1803. They stopped in Clarksville, Indiana to pick up William Clark and additional men. The group left St. Louis, Missouri on May 15, 1804. When they left, Clark was 33, and Lewis was 29.

They spent their first winter among the Mandan tribe in North Dakota, establishing Fort Mandan. It was here that they added French explorer Charbonneau and his wife Sacajawea. They left Fort Mandan in April of 1805, heading up the Missouri river. They reached the Pacific Ocean in November of 1805. The journey would eventually take 28 months and the group would travel 8000 miles.

Cahokia Mounds

T he *Cahokia Mounds* are the largest prehistoric Indian site north of Mexico. The site covers 4000 acres, and contains over 120 mounds. Mounds were made with stone and wood tools. Earth was transported in baskets carried on people's backs, moved from borrow pits to the construction site. Over 50 million cubic feet of earth was moved just for mound construction.

The area was first settled in 700 AD, with the Mississippian culture building highly structured communities by 1000 AD. After 1050 AD, Cahokia became a regional center, reaching its peak in 1050-1200 AD with a population of 10,000 to 20,000 people.

Rectangular platforms were the most common type of platform. They became foundations for ceremonial structures and houses for the elite.

The conical and ridge top mounds at the site were for elite burials. Most Cahokians were buried in cemeteries.

The Monks Mound is the largest prehistoric earthen mound in the Americas, with an estimated 22 million cubic feet. The base is over 14 acres, and the mound rises to 100 feet. A massive building once stood there. The mound was named for the French Monks who lived on a nearby mound from 1809-1813. You will need to climb 156 stairs to get to the top.

One of the most interesting features of the site is Mound 72. During excavations, 300 ceremonial burials were uncovered. The skeletons were mostly young women, and many were in mass graves, and were sacrificed.

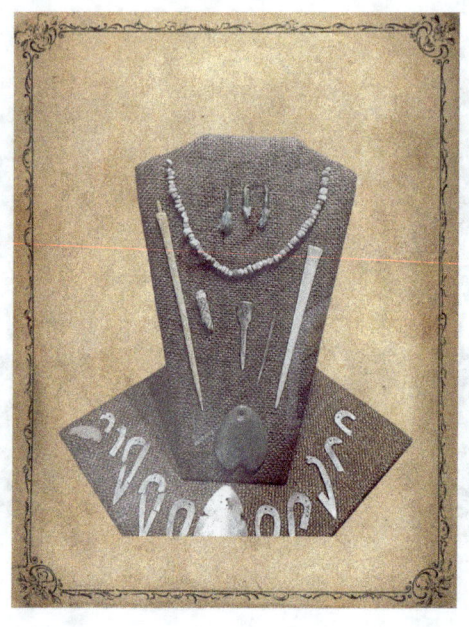

An elite man and woman in their 20s were laid on a deposit of 20,000 marine shell disc beads formed in a raptor bird shape. Nearly 30 percent of the people were non-local immigrants, according to isotope studies.

The site once had a stockade, which is a log wall built for defense. The stockade was 2 miles long and was formed around the central ceremonial area. It was rebuilt four times from 1175-1275 AD.

The site also had a mysterious woodhenge, constructed from 1100-1200 AD. The woodhenge contained five circular sun calendars to determine changing seasons and ceremonial dates.

Cahokia declined beginning in 1200 AD and it was abandoned by 1300 AD. French explorers passed by Cahokia in the 17th century and saw no signs of a settlement. The site is named after the Cahokia tribe, but they didn't arrive until the 1600s.

Don't miss the museum, which contains a wonderful collection of artifacts found at the site. My favorite is this tablet, dating to 1300 AD, found in the Monk's Mound. It is known as the Birdman Tablet, and the image has become the Cahokia Mounds logo.

How to get to the Cahokia Mounds:

The Cahokia Mounds are located at 30 Ramey Street, in Collinsville.

A word about Chunkey:

The game of chunkey, also spelled chungke, was a common entertainment for many cultures, including early inhabitants of Illinois.
The game was played by two men, one of whom rolled a stone
disk, known as a chunkey stone. He and his opponent threw sticks,
known as chungkees, to where they thought the stone would
stop rolling. The one closest to the stone earned points. Chunkey
stones have been found in many sites in the Eastern United States,
often as a grave good.

Fort de Chartres

Massive and magnificent ***Fort de Chartres*** was built in 1720 by the French. The fort is named after Louis, Duc de Chartres, son of the regent of France. The original wooden fort was built in 1718 to 1720. The original fort consisted of a palisade of logs with two bastions at opposite corners for defense.

It became an administrative hub for New France, as the area was known. The fort was also built to help control the Native Americans in the region.

Flooding caused severe damage to the fort, so discussions began in the 1730s to rebuild the fort in stone. Construction of a stone fortress began in 1753 and was completed in 1754, costing an enormous sum of over $1 million dollars. The stone fort had walls 15 feet high and 3 feet thick. Stone was quarried in bluffs nearby and ferried across a lake to the site.

The French gave control of the area containing Fort de Chartres to the British in the 1763 Treaty of Paris. The fort was abandoned by the British in 1772, after a severe flood damaged the fort.

Fort de Chartres fell steadily into ruin, and by 1900, the walls were no longer standing. The ammunition building, known as the magazine, is the only building original to the site. It is thought to be the oldest surviving building in Illinois.

The Catholic chapel, located within the Guard's House, is furnished as it would have looked in the 1750s.

You will also walk through the King's storehouse, which contains the museum. It was originally used to store trade goods before they were moved up and down the Mississippi River.

The museum has a fine collection of artifacts uncovered during excavations. One of my favorite pieces is this lovely key.

During the time of the fort, the Mississippi River was only about 300 yards from the back gate. Trade goods were loaded and un-loaded here.

On December 4, 1803, William Clark of the Lewis & Clark Expedition passed by Fort de Chartres and described the ruins of the fort. Clark was on his way to meet Meriwether Lewis in Cahokia.

How to get to Fort de Chartres:

Fort de Chartres is located at 1350 State Route 155, in Prairie du Roche.

Profiles in history:

William Clark was born August 1, 1770, in Virginia. He was a friendly, extroverted person. After the Lewis and Clark Expedition, Clark became superintendent of Indian affairs in the Louisiana Territory, becoming Governor of Missouri territory in 1810. He died in St. Louis on Sept. 1, 1838, at the age of 68.

Meriwether Lewis was born August 18, 1774. Lewis was a well-educated aristocrat. He became part of the Chosen Rifle Company where he met William Clark. Lewis was expedition leader and asked Clark to join him on the venture. Lewis died in October 1809, suddenly and violently at an inn where he was staying. There is controversy over whether he was murdered or committed suicide. He suffered from depression and consumed alcohol and opium. He was 35.

York was born in 1770 and was William Clark's African American slave. He was responsible for carrying provisions, hunting game, gathering water and performing other tasks for Clark. York was occasionally ordered to dance, which "amused the crowd very much." York was sometimes paraded in front of Native Americans, who marveled at his muscular body and called him "big medicine." After the expedition, York requested to be freed, but Clark refused. He remained a slave until at least 1816, and died of cholera in 1832.

Ghost story:

Fort de Chartres has an interesting ghost story associated with it. A phantom funeral procession was first reported by two women in July, 1889. They saw a line of mourners including at least 40 wagons, 13 groups of soldiers, and a casket, travelling along the road outside of the fort. The procession didn't make a sound. The mourners disappeared near the cemetery outside of town.

There are several incidents which may be the cause of the phantom procession. When the French occupied the garrison, a resident got into an altercation with a soldier, and the resident was killed. The incident was kept quiet, and the man was buried at midnight in the cemetery.

Another incident occurred in 1765, when a French and a British officer got into a duel over a young girl. The British officer died, and the French officer escaped downriver. The British officer was buried quickly and quietly, to avoid problems between the two armies.

The funeral procession is rumored to come to life when three people are on the road to the cemetery, between the hours of eleven and midnight, when July 4th occurs on a Friday.

Pierre Menard Home

The wonderful ***Pierre Menard House*** was the home of Pierre Menard, an early trader. Menard became the first lieutenant governor of Illinois from 1818 to 1822.

The land on which the house stands was purchased in 1802, and construction on the house began the same year. The house is in Southern French Colonial style, furnished with 19th-century period items.

The main floor contains an entry hall, parlor, master bedroom, dining room, two bedrooms, the maid's room, and the nursery.

The stone kitchen is behind the home. Kitchens were often built as separate structures to help prevent fires. There is also a smokehouse, springhouse, and outhouse. You can also enjoy the historic garden.

The grounds once held slave quarters, the location of which was discovered during excavations. Slavery was abolished in Illinois in 1848.

How to get to the Pierre Menard Home:

The Pierre Menard Home is located at 4230 Kaskaskia Road, in Ellis Grove.

Fort Kaskaskia

T he town of *Kaskaskia* was originally established by Jesuit
missionaries in 1703. French settlers began to farm the area,
eventually building a village. Around 1759, the French settlers

built Fort Kaskaskia on the top of a bluff that looked down upon the village. Fort Kaskaskia wasn't actually a fort. It was a system of walls made of earth, to defend against attacks.

Fort Kaskaskia and the surrounding area was given to the British in 1763. In 1778, George Rogers Clark led soldiers down the Ohio River and into the Kaskaskia area. He wished to align himself with French settlers, as a bulwark against the British and their Native American allies. Kaskaskia became part of the United States in the 1783 Treaty of Paris. In 1809, Kaskaskia became the territorial capital of Illinois, and remained so until 1818, when Vandalia was designated the state capital.

Don't miss the Garrison Hill Cemetery, where early settlers of Kaskaskia are buried. The remains of over 3000 people were moved here from Kaskaskia, when flooding threatened several cemeteries in the late 1800s. This cemetery was dedicated in 1891.

How to get to Fort Kaskaskia:

Fort Kaskaskia is located at 4372 Park Road, in Ellis Grove.

Ghost story:

Kaskaskia may suffer from a curse. In 1735, a prosperous French trader lived in Kaskaskia with his daughter. The trader hired both French settlers and Indians to work for him. One of these Indian workers fell in love with the trader's daughter, and she fell in love with him.

The trader fired the Indian and the Indian could no longer find work in the town, so he left. He vowed to come back for his love. The Indian did come back for her, and the two of them escaped to the North. The trader and a few of his friends set off to find the young lovers, which they did. The men tied the Indian to a tree and left him floating down the Mississippi River to drown.

Before he was set adrift, the Indian cast a curse upon everyone. He vowed that the trader would die, and he and his lover would be reunited forever. The town of Kaskaskia would disappear, and the dead in the cemetery would be disturbed from their slumber.

As it happens, the daughter died from starving herself, and the trader was killed in a duel over a business deal. Kaskaskia was flooded by the river, and the bodies of those in the cemetery were washed away.

Shawneetown

T he **Shawneetown Bank** is a magnificent building, built during the years 1839 to 1841. It is the oldest Illinois bank building. The building cost $80,000 to construct. There is a foundation stone listing a date as August 3, 1839, and the bank opened for business in 1841.

Old Shawneetown was known as the gateway to the Illinois Territory, and the commercial center of early Illinois. A federal land office was first established in Old Shawneetown in 1812, allowing settlers to buy and settle land on credit.

The Shawneetown Bank building continued to house various banks up until the 1930s.

How to get to the Shawneetown Bank:

The Shawneetown Bank is located at 280 Washington St, in Shawneetown.

Halfway Tavern

T he ***Halfway Tavern*** is a rustic reconstruction of a tavern which was built here in 1815. The tavern gets its name because it is near the halfway point along the Kaskaskia-Cahokia Trail.

The building was a two-story stagecoach stop frequented by travelers along the trail. The building was both an inn and livery stable.

The building is currently closed to the public, but you can still admire the exterior features, including the cozy windows.

There is a local legend telling of a stagecoach, traveling near the inn in the 1800s. The stagecoach was carrying gold when it was held up by Indians. Before the Indians were caught, they allegedly buried the gold in the forest north of the tavern. The gold has yet to be found, despite numerous searches by local farmers.

How to get to Halfway Tavern:

The Halfway Tavern is located on US Route 50, .5 miles north of Luka.

Favorite Places to Camp

K_askaskia_ has a lovely campground, and it provides the perfect homebase for exploring nearby Fort Kaskaskia, the Pierre Menard Home, and majestic Fort de Chartres. The campground has both primitive tent sites and 32 electric sites, with some available for walk-ins. There are washrooms and running water, but no showers. For reservations, please visit ***ExploreMoreIL*** ™.

Garden of the Gods is a wonderful camping area from which to explore Eastern Illinois. The campground has 12 campsites, tables, fire grills, toilets, drinking water and trails. 6 miles east of Garden of the Gods is ***Pounds Hollow Recreation Area***, which has a campground with 13 electric sites, and 41 non-electric sites. For reservations, please visit ***Recreation.gov***

Random Thoughts
What History Means to Me

First, let me start by sharing with you my opinion of what history isn't. History is not a collection of random dates, names, and places for you to memorize. History is not a dry and uninteresting class you have to pass to graduate.

I believe history is a tangible thing. You can actually *feel* history in the places you go, and the sights you see. I remember walking up to the Acropolis in Athens. I looked down at the well-worn marble steps and wondered about how many ancient philosophers had climbed these very steps, thousands of years ago.

You don't have to go far away to experience the *feeling* of history. If you are lucky enough to live in an old house, you may experience history in your own surroundings. You might say to yourself, *"If only these walls could talk."*

During my travels across the United States, I *felt* history in many, many places. If you travel across the country like I did, you will *feel* the wonderful history of our beautiful country for yourself, and you will never be the same. You will discover what it means to be an American.

Why I travel, and why you should too:

I decided to travel across the country by car because I wanted to rediscover America. When I first set out to explore the history of our country, I wanted to find out why America is the greatest country on earth, and what it means to be an American.

The politics of these United States can be frightening and polarizing. I prefer to focus on what unites us, not what divides us. What unites us is we all live in a spectacularly beautiful country, with warm, wonderful people.

I began my journey five years ago, starting out in my Honda CRV. I soon realized I loved the lifestyle, so now I travel in a small RV. From my small RV, I look out on a country with a unique and colorful, multicultural tapestry, unlike any other country on earth.

I have a degree in Archaeology, and a passion for all things archaeological. I love history, with a side love of paleontology. It is these three passions that I set my trip agenda around. I set out to discover the archaeological sites, history, and paleontological world of our country.

As I travel and write my books, I get asked all the time, especially by women, "What is it like to travel by yourself? Aren't you scared?" The truth is, I believe everyone should do what I did. It's a wonderful way to discover our country, and to rediscover yourself. The truth is, I'm scared not to travel. Traveling allows you to get to know yourself, in ways not possible when sitting on the couch watching TV.

We tend to spend a lot of our lives tuning out the world and our place within it. When you travel, you are quite literally forced to deal with your own thoughts, emotions, and feelings. You can discover yourself while traveling. You can come to understand what makes you who you are, and how you can perhaps become a better person. Above all, traveling gives you mental clarity to figure out how to live with intent. It's a way to guide your life, not just wait for things to happen.

Travel Tips & Stuff

What You Need to Know

How to get started:

Planning your trip should be one of the most exciting things about it. You want to be spontaneous, but it is also very wise to plan your route, so you can take full advantage of all the time and miles you will invest.

- First, decide your passions. If you love airplanes, trains, or old vehicles, plan your trip around that. If you love gardens or architecture, seek that out as the focus of your trip.

- Next, read and research areas of the country that will let you enjoy what you are interested in.

- Make a list by state and city or town, of what you want to see.

- Take your handy road atlas and locate the areas on the pages.

- Make a tentative route plan, so you have an idea of where you are going.

Travel tip: Avoid trying to plan your trip down to a schedule of days, hours, or minutes. On a road trip, it will be virtually impossible to know where you will be on any given day. If you adhere to a schedule, you are more likely to stress out, and less likely to actually enjoy yourself, which is the whole point.

What you need:

You need to bring along a sense of adventure and a curious mind. You need to ditch the idea of always being on a schedule, and live a little more spontaneously to thoroughly enjoy yourself. Things will happen as you travel, both good things and bad things, and you need to prepare your mind and your soul for day-to-day changes.

So much of our lives are planned out. Between growing up, going to school, finding a career, marriage, kids, or whatever, people have lost much of the ability to be spontaneous. But you must take spontaneity on the trip with you, because you may make detours along the way to see something really spectacular.

So, for the practical stuff you need:

*A great vehicle-*I am now five years into the trip and have swapped out my Honda CRV for a small RV, just under 20 feet. I go small because I see humongous RVs on the road, towing a car behind, and all I can think of is, they can't go just anywhere. They are too big. Bad gas mileage, cumbersome to drive, slow, and not agile like my small RV. So, I encourage you, if you want to go car or RV camping and be able to go on remote dirt roads, get an agile vehicle, and small RVs are great.

Travel tip: Don't be afraid to do some modifications to your vehicle. I have made many alterations to my RV, including changing the plumbing, which used to be a mere 4 inches off of the ground, so I would break it all the time. It's now encased in my outside storage compartment. I am also a minimalist, so I have jettisoned anything I won't use or don't love. Don't be afraid to get rid of unnecessary stuff.

An awesome camera that you know inside and out. I use a Nikon and it takes wonderful pictures. Don't skimp on a camera, and don't think a cellphone camera is all you need, because you want the best for your beautiful photos.

Window shades-the best ones are magnetic so you just place them against your windows and they cling to them, obscuring the view inside your car. I also have magnetic window screens, so I can leave my windows down with no bugs!

Battery operated fans and lights-these are important, so you don't have to rely on your house batteries for light and cooling options.

Portable air compressor-this little gem plugs into your cigarette lighter and will inflate your tires if you have a flat. Make sure the air compressor can reach to all of your tires, including your rear tires.

Portable battery charger and power bank-mine comes with battery cables and the power bank, yet once inside the case, it is small enough to put in your glove compartment. This little item, unfortunately, I have had to use, and it saved me.

Portable generator-I have two gas powered generators on the back of my RV, which are hooked together with a coupling unit. I have an interior generator, but after much expense and multiple repairs, it still doesn't work. Now I have generators which will run everything, including AC, and I can maintain them myself.

All season clothing-you never know what different states will bring for weather, so take hot weather and cold weather clothes, and a fair amount of shoes appropriate for hiking, or walking, sandals, and slippers, which are nice at night. Also take along a pair of cheap rubber flip-flops to wear in the public showers you might go into.

Your own pillows-I like my own pillows, so I don't wake up with neck cramps, especially after sleeping in the car.

Sleeping bag and cozy blankets-you want to stay warm and layering is everything.

Warm hat, warm socks, and fuzzy jammies to keep you warm for cold nights sleeping in the car.

A great road atlas, and great guidebooks-get one that's easy to read, with great pictures. For a road atlas, just get one that is easy to read.

A word about photography:

Along with a great camera, you need to have a great eye. This is easier than it sounds once you have worked with your camera and are comfortable taking pictures with it. I am not a professional photographer, but I like my pictures and other people do too.

These are my tips for taking great pictures:

- Experiment with taking both horizontal and vertical shots.

- Don't always put the subject of the photo in the middle of the photograph.

- This one is important: pay attention to the foreground, and if possible, have something, a plant or whatever, in the foreground to help give the photo dimension and depth.

- This one is important too: turn around often to see the view you just came from. I do this quite often and some of my best pictures have resulted from when I turned around and took the shot.

You can also take a mental photo. Place an image in your mind that you can call upon later. Use all of your senses to see, hear, smell, and maybe even to taste, what is around you. You have the means to fully experience your surroundings, and that is very important to a traveler. When you take a mental photo, be sure to jot down quick little details about what you saw, heard, smelled, or tasted, so you can jog your memory later.

And last, but not least...don't be posing in front of everything, everywhere, to show that you actually went somewhere. Most people want to see themselves in your photo and be mentally transported there, but they can't if you are there already.

To camp or not to camp:

Car or RV camping is great. I prefer it to sleeping on the cold, hard ground in a tent. I can lock the doors, put my window shades up and be cozy for the night.

Some people camp in a Walmart parking lot and feel safe. I do not. I believe that if you are in a busy area, you are more likely to be confronted by a nut job who may bother you. Nothing against Walmart, and many Walmart stores don't allow overnight parking. I don't go for rest areas either because they have a track record of incidents happening to people in rest areas, especially women travelers.

I have come to love casino parking lots. I enjoy gambling, so for a little money, many casinos will provide overnight stays if you gamble a little inside the casino. I also do a lot of boondocking, because it's free, and I believe you are safer parked out in the middle of nowhere in the dark.

I also enjoy camping in state or national campgrounds, wildlife sanctuaries, and fairgrounds.

A word about safety:

When you are a woman traveling alone, it's critical to keep a low profile. Don't tell people you are traveling alone, where you are staying, or any other personal information.

I don't go to bars or get drunk. I'm not preaching but you are on your own, in a city or town you've never been to, and you don't know anyone, so it's not the time to lose control of what you are doing. When you are in control, you are better able to decide which people you want to get to know better.

Travel tip: If you feel vulnerable traveling alone, that's OK. Vulnerability is part of passion, and traveling is a passionate thing to do. You can put one of those family stickers on your vehicle to indicate to others that you are not traveling alone, which can help you feel more secure.

Maintain your connections:

When you are traveling alone, there is a definite sense of disconnection. It feels almost like you are the only one in the world, traveling through space and time. That's why it's critical to keep your connections to loved ones active.

Be on Facebook while you are traveling. You may not have internet a lot of the time, or the internet will be poor. Consider paying to have your phone be a hotspot. It's a little bit of money per month, but it's worth it and has saved me from being without internet. I love the convenience of it, and you will too.

Plan your journey around visiting family members or friends you haven't seen for a long time, or people that are good friends. When you see people you know, it will ground you, so you can continue traveling.

Check in by phone with loved ones. They worry about you, and it's good for both of you to stay connected no matter where you are.

Consider traveling with a pet. I now travel with my 12 year-old sheltie Rosie, after losing my beloved sheltie, Sadie. Rosie is a wonderful companion. She is also an excellent watchdog, and barks her head off at other dogs and people.

Travel tip: One of the easiest and best ways I stay connected while traveling is to offer to take a photo for someone I don't know. Many couples, families, or singles would love to have more pictures of themselves traveling. It's an easy and quick way to have a connection with a fellow traveler, and it's good manners too.

Practical matters:

You need to have an address to send your mail to. Keep in touch with whomever is nice enough to do this for you.

You will also need to come back occasionally to register your car, vote, go to doctor visits, and take care of any other business. You can't leave it all behind, as tempting as that may be.

Bad things that happened:

I have had a few problems, mostly associated with my RV. I bought an older model, vintage 1999, and I have had to do a few repairs.

My worst experience came when I took my rig in to a shop in Spokane, Washington (who shall remain nameless.) All I needed was an oil change. I got the oil change and was about an hour south of town on a Friday at 4:30, when my engine blew.

I was in the middle of the eastern Washington prairie, many miles from the nearest town. All I could do was watch my oil drain out onto the Interstate. I can't help but think it was associated with my oil change, but I couldn't prove it. The moral of this story is: DON'T LET JUST ANYONE WORK ON YOUR VEHICLE.

Good things that happened:

I have met many great people on my travels, from all walks of life. I have also learned not to judge people. I have met numerous homeless people who are often just wanting a kind word, and not to be treated like dirt.

People have mistaken me for a homeless person, and I too, have been treated like dirt. When I can, I try to help people and be kind to them. Most of the time, they smile and reciprocate. You will always meet people who are unkind, but they are just as likely to be driving a huge expensive rig, or to be homeless.

We are all Americans, and we are all part of the human race. When you meet people across the country, you realize just how important it is to get to know your fellow citizens, and learn more about how they view the world and our country.

I have to give a special shout-out to the many dedicated people, often volunteers, who staff our state and national parks and monuments. They work tirelessly to ensure the health of our natural resources, and help travelers enjoy their visit. The same is true of the many people who staff the museums in small towns and large cities. They enjoy history, like I do, and it shows in their smiles.

Along with wonderful people, I have seen an America that is spectacularly beautiful, with open prairies, majestic mountains, and crystal clear rivers. I have seen a small fraction of the history of our country. I have seen the memorials to the brave people who shaped our country. I have fallen in love with America in a way that was not possible sitting in my living room. People ask me, "would I do it again?" The answer comes easily, "Yes, in a heartbeat."

Bibliography & Further Reading

America Revealed, 2012, LIFE Books.

Bishop Hill Colony, Illinois Historic Preservation Agency.

Bishop Hill State Historic Site, Illinois Historic Preservation Agency.

Cahokia Mounds State Historic Site, Illinois Department of Natural Resources, 2019.

Finch, etc. al.., Jackie. *Eyewitness Travel USA*. DK Publishing, 2017.

Fort de Chartres, Illinois Historic Preservation Agency.

Fort Kaskaskia & Pierre Menard Home, Illinois Historic Preservation Agency, 2013.

Galena & U.S. Grant Museum, Galena History, 2015.

Iseminger, William, *Cahokia Mounds, America's First City*, The History Press, 2012.

Jones, Landon Y. *The Essential Lewis and Clark*. Harper Collins Publishers, 2000.

Lincoln Home, National Park Service, 2020.

New Salem Village Walking Tour Map.

Peck, David J. *Or Perish in the Attempt: The Hardship and Medicine of the Lewis and Clark Expedition*. The History Press, 2002.

Shenkman,   Richard, Reiger, Kurt, *One-Night Stands with American History*, Harper Collins, 2003.

Silverberg, Robert, *The Mound Builders*, Ohio University Press, 1970.

The Galenian Magazine, Galena Gazette, Fall/Winter 2021-22.

The Old Blacksmith Shop, Galena History.

Thomas, Benjamin, *Lincoln's New Salem*, Southern Illinois University Press, 1982.

Welcome to the Old Lincoln Courtroom and Museum, City of Beardstown.

Index

Referenced by Sections

F

Ford, Harrison-see Famous Illinois Citizens

G

Ghost story-see Lincoln Family Home, Fort de Chartres, Fort Kaskaskia

Grant, Julia-see Galena

Grant, Ulysses S.-see Galena

H

Hearst, William Randolph-see New Salem

Hemingway, Ernest-see Famous Illinois Citizens

Herndon, James & Rowan-see New Salem

Historic Period-see Dickson Mounds

I

Illinois Archaic Period-see Dickson Mounds

J

Jansson, Erik-see Bishop Hill

Jarrot, Nicholas-see Cahokia Village

K

Kiner, Ralph-see Dreams of Illinois

King Louis XV-see Cahokia Village

L

La Pointe-see Galena

Lewis, Meriwether-see Fort de Chartres

Lincoln, Abraham-see Famous Illinois Citizens, Old Lincoln Courthouse, New Salem

M

Menard, Pierre-see Pierre Menard Home

Metzker, James-see Old Lincoln Courthouse

Mississippian Culture-see Cahokia Mounds

Mississippian Period-see Dickson Mounds

Morris, James-see Old Lincoln Courthouse

N

Newhart, Bob-see Famous Illinois Citizens

O

Onstott, Henry-see New Salem

P

Paleo-Indian Period-see Dickson Mounds

Pinet, Father-see Cahokia Village

Profiles in History-see Galena, New Salem, Lincoln Family Home, Cahokia Village, Fort de Chartres

Proto-Historic Period-see Dickson Mounds

S

Sangamon River-see Old Lincoln Courthouse

T

Todd, Mary-see Lincoln Family Home

V

Vaughn, Vince-see Dreams of Illinois

W

Waddell, Martin-see New Salem

White, Betty-see Famous Illinois Citizens

Williams, Robin-see Famous Illinois Citizens

Woodland Period-see Dickson Mounds

Y

York-see Fort de Chartres

About the Author

Julie Bettendorf is a world traveler with a degree in archaeology and a background in history. She has traveled extensively throughout Egypt, Central America, South America, Europe, and the United Kingdom, visiting archaeological and historical sites all along the way.

Currently, Julie is traveling around the US visiting ghost towns, ancient rock art sites, and archaeological wonders as part of research for her ongoing historical travel series entitled ***Wandering Woman***. Wandering Woman is a set of state-by-state guides, full of photographs, historical anecdotes, and unique tips to help other women travel and explore solo across the US by car or RV. Julie enjoys writing freelance blogs, traveling frequently with her two adult children, and hiking outdoors with her faithful dog companion Rosie.

Also by Julie Bettendorf

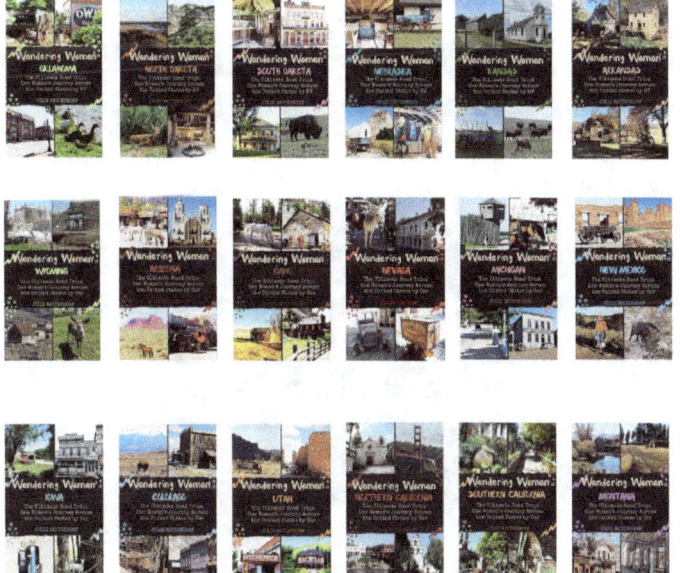

Wandering Woman: Illinois is the most recent book in the *Wandering Woman Travel Series*. Other books in the *Wandering Woman Travel Series* are available in ebook and paperback.

Julie has published two children's books in an ongoing, beautifully illustrated travel series entitled *Anthony Ant Goes to France* and *Anthony Ant Goes to Egypt*.

She has also published a work of historical fiction entitled ***Luxor: Book of Past Lives*** which has recently been released as an audiobook, read by renowned narrator Barry Shannon.